Original title:
Shadows in the Shallows

Copyright © 2025 Creative Arts Management OÜ
All rights reserved.

Author: Vivienne Beaumont
ISBN HARDBACK: 978-1-80587-242-9
ISBN PAPERBACK: 978-1-80587-712-7

Navigating the Twilight Sea

A fish in a tux, such a curious sight,
Dancing through kelp in the dimming twilight.
Jellyfish waltz with a ghostly finesse,
While seaweed giggles in its fuzzy dress.

A crab wearing glasses, it's reading a book,
Telling tall tales of the time it once took.
To the depths where the eels play a game of charades,
While starfish applaud like they're making parades.

The octopus juggles with playful delight,
Swapping his colors from green to blue bright.
All the small fish swim in circles to cheer,
As bubbles explode but they just persevere.

A whale joins the fun, with a laugh so profound,
Tickling the turtles that float all around.
In this goofy realm of marine acrobatics,
Life's one big giggle, full of antics and antics.

The Gloom Beneath the Crest

Bubbles dance like silly feet,
Tickling fish beneath the heat.
A crab in sunglasses waves hello,
While starfish strike a pose in tow.

A splashing seal does a grand dive,
In this funny world, we thrive.
With each ripple, giggles arise,
As dolphins plot their silly highs.

Dim Echoes of the Resounding Sea

Whales hum tunes of wacky cheer,
While seaweed flirts with passing deer.
An octopus juggles old boots,
To the rhythm of ocean roots.

Turtles in bow ties dance so slow,
Doing the cha-cha with a glow.
Mermaids laugh with watery grace,
Splashing joy in this merry place.

Figures in the Murky Blue

A ghostly fish with googly eyes,
Sneaks a peek, then takes to the skies.
A pirate cat with a wooden tail,
Swings on bubbles, tells a tall tale.

Squid wear hats, quite out of style,
While clowns fish and swim with a smile.
In silly wigs, they frolic around,
Creating laughs without a sound.

Resonance of the Abyssal Light

Angler fish shows off a bright grin,
While guppies join in for a spin.
A lobster plays on a tiny drum,
Drawing in friends with a funny hum.

Glowing plankton dance in delight,
Every flicker feels just right.
With laughter lurking in the deep,
Ocean secrets are ours to keep.

Murmurs in Twilight

In the dusk, the crabs all dance,
Wiggling sideways, what a chance!
Fish gossip while they munch on algae,
Under the moon, it's a real grand party.

Eels play tag in the slipping light,
Yelling 'Catch me!' with all their might.
Starfish throw confetti in the sea,
Who knew they were so extra, you see?

A turtle laughs at a clownfish's joke,
As bubbles rise, we all get choked.
An octopus plays the saxophone,
While seaweed sways, all alone.

So come and join this crazy spree,
Where laughter bubbles, wild and free.
In this twilight, the moves are slick,
The ocean's groove is quite the trick!

Secrets of the Deep

Underwater whispers, oh so bright,
Clams giggle with all their might.
Anemones wave in silly cheers,
While dolphins chuckle, easing fears.

Crabs wear hats made of fronds,
Dancing to their own little songs.
A flounder slips out for a snack,
In this fun world, there's no lack.

Sea horses, proud in a conga line,
With a twist and a turn, they look divine.
A grouper jokes, 'Why the long face?'
With a splash, they're off in a race.

So dive on down, don't be shy,
In the watery dance, we'll all fly high.
Secrets abound in the deep abyss,
Where laughter and joy are hard to miss!

Reflections on the Fringe

Dancing light on waves so wide,
Fishes flash and glide with pride.
Bubbles rise, giggling with glee,
What silly antics, oh can't you see?

A puffer fish poofs with flair,
While a jellyfish floats without a care.
A sea cucumber tumbles in glee,
Who knew they had such lively esprit?

In the limelight, a crab pulls a face,
Chasing after a small, quick trace.
A clownfish can't stop cracking jokes,
While starfish laugh behind their pokes.

So let's reflect beneath the wave,
Where joy and mirth are all we crave.
In the fringe of the ocean's play,
Let's giggle and splash 'til end of day!

Hues of Dimness

In the hue of dim, things get wild,
A flatfish grins, looking so styled.
Corals swirl, in colors so bright,
While a sea urchin beams with delight.

The moonbeams play tag on the floor,
As an old turtle tells tales of lore.
Fishy friends join in for a laugh,
Creating chaos on their underwater path.

Lanternfish twinkle like stars in the sea,
With a wink and a smile, oh so free.
An octopus juggles shells with a cheer,
Amidst the fun, there's nothing to fear.

For dimness holds treasures galore,
In this underwater scene we adore.
Let's twirl and swirl, join in the spree,
As the ocean sings its harmony!

Calmness Amidst the Chaos

In the pool, a fish named Lou,
Wore a hat and glasses too.
He danced around with quite a flair,
As seahorses giggled in mid-air.

Crabs clapped claws in joyous cheers,
While a turtle caught all the sneers.
Bubbles popped with every joke,
As octopuses did a little poke.

The current swirled like a fun ride,
With all his pals right by his side.
A whirlpool formed to music's beat,
And everybody moved their feet.

So in the chaos, all could find,
A splash of joy, a twist of mind.
For laughter echoes through the wave,
In watery realms, fun is brave!

Tides of Translucence

Oysters held an oyster ball,
With glittering shells, they dressed up all.
The clownfish juggled seaweed snacks,
While conchs played tunes that broke their backs.

Bubble-blowers side by side,
Lost their breath, but laughed with pride.
A disco ball made of a pearl,
Twinkled bright in an underwater whirl.

Starfish twirled, a ballet grand,
A dance unique, no touch of sand.
The sea green lights sparkled bright,
As fishes winked in sheer delight.

At ebb and flow, the joy was clear,
In every wave, there lurked a cheer.
For underneath the watery dome,
Laughter ruled, and all felt home!

Remarks from the Depths

A wise old eel, with tales galore,
Whispered secrets from the ocean floor.
His stories made the fish all laugh,
Though most would miss the hidden gaff.

A dolphin joined, with jokes on queue,
While flounders flipped, oh, what a view!
"Why do the sea cucumbers creep?"
"Because they dream of a leap, a leap!"

The sea turtles rolled, a comic show,
As anemones swayed, stealing the glow.
With laughter echoing through the reefs,
The currents danced, and joy was chief.

In depths below, where dark things hide,
Humor thrived as the fates tied.
And from the depths, not one could fret,
For fishy banter was the best bet!

Quietude in the Crescendo

In ripples soft, the laughter flowed,
With muffled giggles, the rhythm glowed.
A starfish wearing a tiny crown,
Adored by all in the sea town.

Turtles spinning in oodles of glee,
While krill applauded, as boisterous as can be.
A singular clam, who loved to show,
Dropped a pearl, "It's my disco glow!"

With currents wild, they broke the calm,
A flowing tide, a seaweed balm.
The fish in robes of coral bright,
Joined in harmony 'neath the moonlight.

So as the echoes surged and soared,
Every wave saw joy restored.
In quietude where laughter thrived,
The fun beneath was truly alive!

The Weave of Water and Shade

Bubbles dance beneath the dock,
Fishes giggle, who'll take stock?
Mermaids prance with silly glee,
All while ducks play hide and seek.

A gopher grins, peeks from a hole,
Whispers secrets, half a droll.
The otters slip upon the wet,
Sending every catfish to fret.

Twinkling lights on the water's face,
Water lilies join the race.
Crickets chirp their nightly tune,
As frogs croak jokes to the moon.

Waves clap hands, the ripples cheer,
Every splash a silly jeer.
In this world of wink and jest,
The weave of life is at its best!

Sorting Through the Half-Lights

Mice with capes run on the ledge,
Hiding snacks by the old hedge.
Fireflies looking quite bemused,
Playing games while they get schooled.

A cat in pajamas yawns and sighs,
Caught by surprise beneath the skies.
Twinkling stars dance a merry jig,
As the moon joins with a prance so big.

A turtle slips, but then rescues toast,
In the water, it makes quite the boast.
Silly sounds echo through the night,
Chasing shadows just out of sight.

With laughter that floats on the breeze,
Even fish share secrets with ease.
Sorting echoes of frogs' banter,
While crickets in harmony start to canter.

Elderberries by the Shore

Elderberries float, looking quite spry,
As raccoons throw a party nearby.
Laughter bubbles, splashes abound,
In the sunset, such joy can be found.

A seagull tries to steal a pie,
While a clam shells out a goofy sigh.
Turtles waddle in jovial haste,
Turning the shoreline into a feast.

Jellyfish swing with capricious flair,
While barnacles gossip without a care.
Sandy toes find rhythm in sand,
As the ocean makes room for the band.

With a wink and a splash, they retreat,
As tides bring dances to the beat.
Elderberries laugh as they sway,
Celebrating life in their own way!

Incognito at Dusk

At dusk, all critters don their disguise,
A frog in a hat, oh what a surprise!
Raccoons wear shades with a nifty style,
Giggling together, it's all worthwhile.

A snail in a scarf finds his groove,
While a crab breaks out his best dance move.
Under the cover of the moonlight's grin,
The party starts, let the fun begin!

Will-o'-the-wisps sneak a peek,
As owls hoot out a humorous cheek.
The fireflies twinkle with glee and flair,
Illuminating the mischief in the air.

With laughter shared over glowing tea,
Creatures commingle as wild as can be.
Incognito, they relish this dusk,
Comedic tales fuel the joyous musk!

Beneath the Lapping Waves

Tiny fish swim with great flair,
While crabs do pirouettes without a care.
Bubble-blowing seaweed in a twist,
Making waves is quite the humorous gist.

Starfish giggle on their rocky perches,
As ocean's laughter chimes through the searches.
A seagull swoops in for a sandwich tease,
While barnacles sing in their cozy breeze.

Veiled Apparitions at Dusk

Glimmers of light on the shore do prance,
As creatures prepare for their twilight dance.
Oysters wearing costumes made of shells,
Telling jokes that only the sea dwells.

The moon winks, a mischievous ghost,
While crabs in tuxedos make quite the boast.
With jellyfish twirls and a splashy bow,
The humor of night makes the sea take a vow.

Unseen Dancers of the Coast

Whirlpools spinning tales of light,
While fish in tuxedos take to flight.
A dolphin giggles as it does flip,
In this undersea party, there's no need to trip.

Clams clap their shells in rhythmic beats,
Eels do the hustle on slippery seats.
Sand dollars roll in with a sly little grin,
As laughter and mischief surely begin.

Half-Remembered Ghosts of the Harbor

In the cobwebs of tide, a riddle hides,
Waves chuckling softly as mischief abides.
Old boats croak jokes as they sway with glee,
Whilst fish play tag, as happy as can be.

Forgotten flotsam has tales to spin,
Of mermaid parties where the laughter's been.
With nets full of giggles and waves full of cheer,
The harbor's a place where fun draws near.

Beneath the Glimmering Waves

Fish wear snorkels, quite absurd,
They giggle as they take a turn.
Octopus in plaid, a real trend,
Flip-flops on, they dance and bend.

Crabs pulling pranks, watch them go,
Stealing treasures, oh what a show!
Seaweed sways, a wild hairdo,
Under the waves, a laugh or two.

Starfish in hats, what a sight!
Jellyfish join, glowing at night.
Bubbles burst with a gentle cheer,
Under the glimmer, fun is near.

A dolphin spins, a comic act,
While clams play cards, quite a pact.
Let's dive deep for joy and jest,
In this watery world, we're all blessed.

Silhouettes in the Stillness

A seahorse winks, a cheeky greet,
A hermit crab relocates his seat.
Clams gather round for gossip and cheer,
Echoing laughter, it's crystal clear.

A whale sings low, a tune so wrong,
Fish join in, humming along.
Coral reefs sway like they're in a dance,
Turtles chuckle, it's their chance.

Deep in the blue, an anchor's misplaced,
Bubbles of laughter, no time to waste.
Dancing sea creatures lit by the moon,
In the stillness, we all croon.

What's that? A crab trying to tease?
Wiggling and jiggling, oh what a breeze!
Laughter erupts from the depths below,
Join in the fun, let your joy flow.

Lurking in the Light

A glowworm shines, with a silly grin,
While fish play tag, round and round they spin.
Lobsters in tuxes, ready to dine,
Crack jokes and giggles, oh so divine!

A light ray beams, gives a wink,
As sharks do the cha-cha, what do you think?
Anemones giggle, tickled by rays,
It's a laugh fest, in these fun-filled bays.

Eels with bow ties slithering by,
Throwing a party, oh me, oh my!
Bubble-blowing contests, make a big mess,
With wit and charm, they all impress.

As the sun sets, hues mix and blend,
A dance of the sea, where laughter won't end.
In the light's embrace, we all unite,
In this world of glee, everything feels right.

Depths of Half-Light

Down in the depths, the mirth unfolds,
With fish so bright, and stories told.
A clownfish cracks jokes without a care,
While cobwebs of light dart here and there.

Crabs in sunglasses, looking so cool,
Do the shuffle, they're breaking the rule.
With sea cucumbers doing the twist,
Their dance moves, you just can't resist.

The anglerfish grins, with a shining lure,
While sea otters munch, their giggles endure.
In this quirky world of splash and sway,
We find our joy in a playful way.

Manta rays glide, with grace and style,
In soft half-light, they chat for a while.
Laughter echoes, a watery delight,
In the depths below, the fun feels so right.

Whispers Beneath the Surface

In the depths where fish play hide,
A giggle from the seaweed slides.
A crab takes up a dance in glee,
Waving claws like it's a spree.

Bubbles burst with jokes untold,
Clownfish act so brave and bold.
They practice moves that make you laugh,
As sea turtles do the math.

A starfish yells, 'I'm quite the star!'
But really just a mini car.
With all the quirks and funny sights,
It's endless fun beneath the lights.

So dive below and take a peek,
At all the silly things they speak.
With laughter ringing through the brine,
Each moment here is quite divine.

Silhouettes of Forgotten Dreams

In twilight's soft and dreamy glow,
Figures dance, but move too slow.
A fish in socks skims by the reef,
A finned comedian, oh, so brief.

They mime their tales of treasure lost,
Draw maps with chalk at noon's great cost.
An octopus wears a silly hat,
Says, 'No one notices, imagine that!'

Behind the rocks, a turtle snores,
Dreaming big of ocean shores.
With giggles soft and echoes keen,
A water world that's quite the scene.

So watch and laugh, oh what a sight,
These wavy forms in fading light.
Forgotten dreams come out to play,
In funny ways, they pass the day.

Echoes in the Tidal Pools

In pools where crabs and snails convene,
Echoes bounce in a bubbling sheen.
A fish tells tales in wobble speech,
While others practice their own screech.

Barnacles gather, gossip flies,
While starfish search for the right ties.
They flip and flop in a blushing fit,
Claiming seaweed is the ultimate hit.

With shells as hats and pebbles whole,
The sea's oddball comedy takes a toll.
A jellyfish jigs in the gentle sway,
As laughter ripples and frolics play.

So join the fun, let spirits soar,
In tidal pools, there's so much more.
Where every wave and splash provides,
A chance to dance where humor hides.

Reflections of the Dusk Tide

As dusk descends on the wavy ward,
A dolphin cracks a joke, quite forward.
It leaps and flips with a wink and grin,
While fishes roll their eyes in sin.

The sand's alive with whispering sound,
As clams and mussels gather 'round.
They trade puns and a little slap,
In this sea-based comedy trap.

An eel appears, with humor sly,
Says, 'I've got nothing but waves to fly.'
While bubbles rise with laughter loud,
Their fun grows bolder, and they're so proud.

In twilight's glow, shenanigans spark,
Where bubbles dance and giggles mark.
Reflections ripple in a joyous tide,
With comedy swimming side by side.

Facets of Fading Light

In the twilight glow, laughter stirs,
With wiggly fish and sneaky blurs.
They dance in bubbles, a slippery play,
Tickling the surface, they giggle away.

A crab with shades, struts with pride,
Waves a claw like a knight on a ride.
He shuffles sideways on his own parade,
While the minnows tease, and the seaweed swayed.

Glints of mischief from aquatic friends,
In the murky depths, where hilarity blends.
A lost sock floats, quite the sight,
Turns out it's just the sea's delight.

The sun dips low, the giggles rise,
The fish swim close, under sea-silk skies.
With silly pranks, they splash and dart,
Life in the waters, a whimsical art.

Beneath the Surface's Embrace

In murky waters, a joke's afloat,
Where turtles coast in a whimsical boat.
Starfish giggle, a silent cheer,
Their arms wave wildly, it's quite the sphere.

A clam starts to drum, with shells so bright,
The octopus dances, oh what a sight!
With wobbly moves and a wiggly grin,
They throw a party, let the fun begin!

Small fish tease with a flick and a flash,
While the seaweed sways in a joyful clash.
They tag the old eel, quite the sly prank,
He swirls in circles, then gives a honk.

Bubbles rise up, with laughter entwined,
All creatures gather, joyfully inclined.
With each splash and giggle, the ocean calls,
Beneath the surface, humor enthralls.

The Elusive Depths

In the depths below where mysteries twirl,
A wise old turtle spins in a whirl.
He tells fish tales, both funny and bold,
Of lost treasure and shrimp, oh so old.

A mackerel slips on a slippery midge,
Causing a scene at the coral ridge.
With giggles and splashes, they roll and sway,
While seahorses sigh, it's just their way.

A jellyfish floats, with a wobbly glee,
Saying, "Watch me, watch me! Come swim with me!"
They twirl and they jiggle, in glimmering light,
Playing tag with the moonbeams, what a sight!

The clock ticks slow, but the laughter's fast,
Waves carry giggles from the present to past.
In waters deep, where time takes a leap,
Fun and folly, what secrets they keep.

Interwoven Threads of Dusk

Threads of twilight weave a funny tale,
With fishy pranks amidst the gentle swell.
A school of guppies in a synchronized dance,
Wiggling and jiggling, they leap at a chance.

The fading light casts a mischievous grin,
As crabs play poker, let the games begin!
Cards made of seaweed, a diamond in sight,
Clinking their claws, it's a hilarious fight.

Worms wearing hats made of fine sea glass,
Skim through the shallows, hoping to pass.
They flip and they flop, but tumble instead,
Rolling in laughter, while others just fled.

As day begins fading, the antics ensue,
With friends in the water where whimsy rings true.
In a twilight of mirth, they splash all around,
In the soft, shimmering dusk, laughter is found.

Conspiracies beneath the Blue

Fish in tuxedos plotting schemes,
Whispers carried under moonbeams.
Crabs wearing hats, they shifty glance,
Dance in circles like it's a trance.

Octopuses nod with sly grins,
Trading secrets with the fins.
Jellyfish in neon coats,
Spin tall tales like merry boats.

Faint Flickers in the Water

Bubbles rise with giggles bright,
Flopping fish in sheer delight.
Glimmers chase the playful tease,
While snails play tag with perfect ease.

Wobbling seaweed waves a hello,
Nudging clams that shuffle slow.
A starfish twirls in silly pride,
As bubbles burst with joyous ride.

Interludes of the Abyss

Deep down where light takes a nap,
A ghostly eel waves in a flap.
Sea cucumbers tell silly jokes,
While clownfish swim with punchy pokes.

Turtles wear sunglasses, real cool,
And join the parade, gathering a school.
Electric rays dance with a jolt,
Painting the dark with a humorous bolt.

Rippled Reveries

Mermaids giggle at silly sights,
Comets are fish with glowing lights.
Tangled seaweed that sings along,
With dolphins splashing a silly song.

Anemones sway with a playful wink,
Pufferfish puffed in a link.
Frolicking whispers below the tide,
Where laughter of creatures cannot hide.

Eclipsed by Wetness

A frog leapt high in a splashy jest,
Turning puddles to mirrors, he felt like the best.
A duck quacked loud, with a waddle so proud,
While rain danced in beats, quite noisy and loud.

They slipped and they slid, in a comical race,
With glee on their faces, pure joy in the place.
But a tumble in mud turned their laughter to squeals,
As they rolled in the muck, oh, what silly appeals!

From Gloom to Glimmer

A cat in a hat, with a twitch of its tail,
Stalks shadows of bugs on a dusky pale trail.
With a pounce and a leap, it trips over a shoe,
In the gloomiest light, laughter bursts through.

A dog with a grin, chased the mysterious tail,
Rolling over in leaves, as if in a sail.
Gloom faded away as they danced in delight,
In a spark of pure fun during soft twilight.

The Quiet Between Us

In whispers of night, while the crickets all chirp,
Two friends sat in silence, sharing a smirk.
A sudden loud splash, made them both jump up,
It was just a big fish, seeking just one more cup.

They chuckled and gasped, then burst into fits,
As the fish would pop up and perform funny tricks.
With laughter alight, they forgot all their woes,
'Cause in moments like these, friendship only grows.

Subtle Shapes at Dusk

A squirrel danced round on a thin little wire,
Pretending to tightrope, a creature of fire.
While below in the grass, a mouse took its stand,
With a tip of its cap, as if part of the band.

The shapes they did make, in the dim evening light,
Were a funny ballet, quite a whimsical sight.
A laugh from a breeze, as the dusk softly sighed,
In the theater of dusk, with giggles, they cried.

Cast Away Dreams

On a sandy shore, a flip-flop lies,
A lone fish swims while a seagull cries.
A hermit crab in a tiny shell,
Is plotting his move, oh what the hell!

The tide rolls in with a giggle and sway,
Tickling the toes of folks at play.
A beach ball bounces, a wild chase starts,
As laughter echoes, it steals our hearts.

A sunburnt lobster in shades so bright,
Claims he's the king of the sun's golden light.
With a wave of his claw, he struts and sways,
Declaring each sunset is truly his praise.

So let's toss our worries in the deep blue sea,
Dance with the waves, let the day be free.
With crabs on parade and fish in a race,
Who knew the beach could be such a place?

Fathoms of Forgotten Tales

Down in the deep, where the fish tell lies,
A goggle-eyed squid dreams of butterfly flies.
With a wink and a wave of his tentacle bold,
He spins wild yarns that never get old.

A sock-eyed salmon swims in a dress,
Hoping to catch the waves with finesse.
His friends all chuckle, it's quite the show,
As he twirls and spins with a dazzling glow.

A clam in the sand plays a game of chess,
With a crab named Larry, it's anyone's guess.
Each move a giggle, their laughter rings,
Who knew that clams had such clever wings?

With bubbles of joy and giggles untold,
These fanciful fish share secrets of old.
Dive in with a splash that brings smiles anew,
In the fathoms of fun, there's magic for you!

The Mists that Cloak

In the early morn, when the fog rolls in,
Seagulls squawk loudly, they're ready to win.
A fisherman trips on his own tangled net,
As fishy jokes slip through the mist like a pet.

A ghostly whale sings a tune to the breeze,
While dolphins perform, they dance with such ease.
The foghorn moans, a melodic surprise,
As misty shenanigans twinkle in eyes.

An octopus whispers on a coral chair,
Telling tall tales of those who dared.
With a pinch of humor and a sprinkle of charm,
He leaves all around him safe from any harm.

So here in the mists, laughter takes flight,
With sea creatures joining, what a delightful sight.
In the cloak of the dawn, with giggles we stroll,
Finding magic in moments that brighten the soul!

Chiaroscuro of the Coast

On a canvas of azure, the sun takes a dive,
Mermaids are painting, oh how they thrive!
With brushes of kelp and colors so bright,
Each splash is a giggle, a dream in the light.

A lighthouse beams, keeping secrets at bay,
As creatures below dance the night away.
With laughter as their rhythm, they twirl in delight,
Under moons that shimmer, under stars that ignite.

A seal takes a selfie, what a sight to see,
With a cheesy grin, he's as happy as can be.
While crabs keep on crabwalking in comical form,
Their sideways adventures are lively and warm.

Chiaroscuro of the coast shines with glee,
A playful reminder of how fun life can be.
With every tide turning and laughter in tow,
Join the parade where the silly fish glow!

When the Tide Stirs

The sea laughed loud, a playful hum,
Came a crab with a dance, oh so dumb.
He twirled his claws, a wobbly spree,
While seagulls cackled, full of glee.

The waves tickled toes, what a sight!
A fish wore a hat, oh what a fright!
Paddling about, without a care,
Bubbly giggles floated in the air.

A dog in a wave, he tried to swim,
But ended up splashing, looking grim.
With a flick of his tail, he dashed away,
Leaving behind a soggy ballet.

The tide rolled back, with a wink so sly,
As shells chuckled softly, oh me, oh my!
In this funny dance of light and foam,
The ocean whispers, "You're never alone!"

Fog-Laden Whispers

In the morning mist, what a sight,
A clam told a joke, oh what a fright.
A starfish exclaimed, "I've lost my grip!"
As bubbles giggled in a wondrous trip.

The fog rolled in, all thick and grey,
A fish with a monocle joined the fray.
He cleared his throat, gave a grand speech,
While seaweed swayed, eating each peach.

A squid tried to waltz, but slipped on a rock,
"Watch where you're going!" the octopus cocks.
They tumbled and rolled in a comical way,
Making the morning a slapstick play.

As the fog lifted, they cheered with delight,
All creatures of water, what a funny sight!
With laughter that bubbled, the day felt so bright,
The sea's gentle humor, a pure delight.

Dim Reflections

In the twilight glow, a fin did prance,
A fish with a hat took a chance.
He tiptoed through weeds, looking for fun,
While shadows behind him decided to run.

A gnome made of driftwood grinned with glee,
Much to the surprise of a curious bee.
"Why do you stare?" chirped the little bug,
As the sun's rays danced, giving a hug.

And who's that lurking near the rocks?
A crab with a whip, training to box!
With a swing and a pinch, he put on a show,
While fish cheered loud, "Go, go, go!"

As day turned to night, all creatures dispersed,
With a wink and a wave, for laughter they thirst.
In the dimming light, the fun lingered still,
In pools of reflection, the water's sweet thrill.

Glistening Mermaids

In the moonlit bay, they twirled with glee,
Glistening mermaids, so wild and free.
With shells in their hair and fish in a line,
They laughed at the world, feeling just fine.

A bubble burst forth, tickling a toe,
As a fish played the lute, stealing the show.
"Join us at sunset, wear your best smile!"
The waves echoed back, stretching a mile.

One mermaid tripped, went head over tail,
As everyone squealed, "Oh, tell us the tale!"
Flipping and flopping, they danced like mad,
For the night was young, and they all felt glad.

They splashed and they played until morning's light,
Whispering secrets in the shimmering night.
With giggles aplenty and laughter so sweet,
These glistening legends will never admit defeat.

Ripples of the Unspoken Past

In the depths of the gentle tide,
Old secrets giggle and slide.
A crab in a hat, winks at a fish,
"I knew your grandmother, quite the swish!"

Nautical tales swirl in the breeze,
As clams play cards, doing just as they please.
The wave whispers jokes to the silent moon,
While driftwood dances, making quite the tune.

A seagull with glasses squints near a shell,
Says, "I've got gossip, it's juicy and swell!"
The ocean grins wide, a jester at play,
As starfish flip coins, betting their day.

So join the mirth of the tides so sly,
Where laughter floats low and spirits fly high.
Each ripple a chuckle, each foam a cheer,
In the watery world, where fun's always near.

Starlit Figures Along the Shore

Beneath the moon, the dancers emerge,
Octopuses tango, a wiggly surge.
A clam in a tutu leads the parade,
While jellyfish bob like a neon charade.

Starfish play poker, the stakes are high,
With shells for chips, they shoot and they sigh.
The tide rolls in with a tumble and flip,
And dolphins join in for a synchronized trip.

A crab in a tux gives a wink and a nudge,
"Who says crustaceans can't hold a grudge?"
As the laughter grows, the sand starts to laugh,
Turning shells into jokes, a natural craft.

In this seaside gala, where secrets comply,
The figures shimmer, the hours slip by.
Under the stars, where the fun doesn't cease,
Life's just a dance, a wavy caprice.

Enigmas of the Shimmering Foam

Bubbles pop secrets like fizzing wine,
As sea cucumbers plot over brine.
A dolphin with glasses reads fish gossip,
While seaweed sways to a groovy bip.

The foam whispers tales of the silly and bold,
Of turtles in glasses, and antics retold.
With every crest, a chuckle is cast,
As fish in bow ties swim far too fast.

A shrimp with a mic takes center stage,
Cracking corny jokes, acting his age.
The snails roll their eyes, but still can't resist,
Cackling together at a punchline twist.

In this luminous mix, where mischief does loom,
The foamy enigmas create a sweet gloom.
So let's toast to the laughter that bubbles and swirls,
In the dance of the sea, with its playful whirls.

Glimmers of Ancients Beneath

In the depths where the sunbeams wane,
Ancient toys float, released from the mundane.
A shipwrecked rubber duck lets out a quack,
Proclaiming, "I'm the captain! You'll never look back!"

Rocky neighbors roll with the tide,
Sardines in tuxedos, swimming with pride.
A wooden leg laughs at the pirate's frolic,
"Yo-ho, me hearties, history's symbolic!"

The kraken's old tales whispered low with glee,
Of mermaids who danced, wild and free.
As treasures chuckle and softly collide,
Each glimmering secret becomes their guide.

So dive into depths where the laughter's at play,
Where ancient spirits still dance in the bay.
With bubbles of humor and currents of cheer,
The past waves hello, bringing fun ever near.

The Haunting Beneath the Bay

There once was a fish with a sense of flair,
He wore a top hat and danced without care.
The crabs all applauded, they shouted with glee,
"What a grand ocean party! Let's all swim with glee!"

Late in the night, when the tide got quite low,
A squid with a mustache put on a grand show.
He juggled some pearls while the lobsters all laughed,
What a sight to behold, it was quite a craft!

As eels in tuxedos swam round in a spree,
They spritzed all the jellyfish, giggling with glee.
But then out came a shark looking rather perplexed,
"Why do you party? This place is context!"

The fish in the deep just waved him goodbye,
"Join us next time, dear friend, don't be shy!"
And so through the bay, laughter echoed each night,
A carnival under the moon, what a sight!

Trivia in the Twilight

The octopus posed a riddle so sly,
"What has eight arms, and drinks coffee? Oh my!"
The fish rolled their eyes and they pondered around,
Till one said, "It's you! When your jokes rebound!"

A dolphin chimed in, with mischief and cheer,
"What swims in a circle and drinks lots of beer?"
The answer was simple, they all knew it well,
It's a fish with a keg, and it surely can tell!

As night fell over the waves, full of fun,
A parrotfish shouted, "Let's all start to run!"
They raced to the surface in laughter and light,
Chasing first stars that twinkled so bright!

In the twilight, they danced with a skip in their tail,
With trivia games, there was no chance to fail.
And as they all frolicked beneath the night skies,
They giggled and grinned with delight in their eyes!

Mystic Waters' Secrets

In mystical waves where the secrets now play,
An eel wore a crown made of seaweed one day.
He tricked all the fish into thinking he's king,
"Bow to my presence; let the praises all sing!"

A turtle with glasses, quite slow, and astute,
Said, "Dear little eel, you look cute in that suit!"
The fish all erupted in giggles and glee,
As they danced in the bubbles and swam wild and free.

With tales of enchantment from driftwood and kelp,
The shrimp spun stories that made the seas melt.
"Did you hear about Larry? He wore a pink hat!"
"Rumor has it he challenged a cat!"

The currents laughed loudly; there's joy in the depths,
Where secrets are told in hilarious steps.
So if ever you wander near murky lanes,
Just know that the fun here will tickle your brains!

The Underlying Abyss

In the depths of the sea, where the fish go to chill,
A dolphin once stocked up on sea snacks until—
He tripped on a starfish, it flipped with a spin,
And danced on the waves with a corkscrew-like grin!

There once was a crab who loved telling tall tales,
Of treasure and pirates and old rusty gales.
When asked where he got all his fanciful lore,
He just smirked and hid a few gems on the shore!

An old whale blew bubbles while cracking some jokes,
About crusty old barnacles and silly sea folks.
The otters were rolling, they just couldn't cope,
With puns that were lighter than a floating soap!

Yet deep in the waters, where laughter ignites,
No worries can linger, no serious sights.
They revel in antics beneath waves up high,
For beneath every wave, there's a funny fish guy!

A Dance with the Dusk

When daylight fades, the giggles grow,
A moonlit jig, with a toe-tapping show.
The crabs in tuxedos, they strut and sway,
While fish all laugh and dance in play.

Twinkling lights on the watery floor,
Invite the shrimp to join in for more.
With every splash, a bubble of cheer,
As laughter echoes, it's clear we're near.

The starfish spins in a clumsy round,
As jellyfish float, they're barely bound.
Who knew this party was quite so bright?
A dance with the dusk, oh what a sight!

So let's tiptoe lightly, avoid the squawks,
For crabs might pinch if we laugh and gawk.
In the darkness, a funny parade,
As secrets danced 'neath the ocean's cascade.

Glistening Ghosts

In the depths where the silly fish joke,
The bubbles rise with a soft, funny poke.
A glowing eel tells tales with a grin,
Of daring fish and the losses they win.

Glistening wonders, they wiggle and shake,
While anchovies craft a scene by the lake.
With laughter afloat and silliness rife,
Every fin flaunts a comical life.

Witty whispers ride on the tide,
As giggling minnows swim side by side.
The jellyfish twirl, a translucent jest,
In a glimmering land where all are blessed.

So come, take a dip in this frothy spree,
Where fish giggle and dance like you and me.
A world of delight beneath the gloss,
With glistening ghosts and their humorous toss.

Submerged Silences

With every ripple, a chuckle is born,
In a world where the quiet are never forlorn.
The clams all giggle with shells shut tight,
While the seaweed jokes in the warm twilight.

Bubbles arise, like secrets set free,
As laughter drifts down in a silvery spree.
A turtle winks at the drifting fluff,
In a trickster's realm, there's always enough.

Fishy debates happen just out of reach,
As sand dollars lecture like they're at a beach.
The corals chuckle in vibrant tune,
With underwater gags that make us swoon.

In the depths where the whispers play cool,
With issues as light as a conch shell's rule.
Submerged silences aren't always bland,
In this giggly world, quite humorously planned.

Veiled Visions

Through the water's veil, a playful day,
Where fish wear glasses in a curious way.
A sieve of giggles drifts through the tide,
As visions old and funny collide.

A school of sillies swim in a line,
Swapping tall tales about fish and brine.
With a wink and a nod, they swim out of view,
But not without leaving a chuckle or two.

Eels in a twist all tease the crab king,
As bubbles burst and the sea starts to sing.
The dolphins leap high, with a splash and a cheer,
Creating a party for all those who dare.

Veiled visions dance like a comical mirage,
Where every fin flips with an elegant collage.
In a world vast and gleefully wide,
In the ocean's embrace, we joyfully ride.

Dreams that Sink

In the depths where giggles hide,
Dreams take a plunge, oh what a ride!
Mermaids laugh with fins so spry,
While seaweed waves a goofy bye.

A sunken treasure full of smiles,
Grinning crabs dance for miles and miles!
Each bubble bursts with silly sounds,
As fish in tuxes swim 'round in bounds.

No worries here, just guffaws galore,
As jellyfish float and gently soar.
Chasing a dream that's lost in play,
In the best of depths, we'll backstroke all day.

So dive right in, let laughter leak,
In these giddy depths, we're on a streak!
Forget the worries, and bring a grin,
In this watery world, let fun begin!

Currents of Obscurity

Waves of goofiness swirl around,
Where lost socks form a silly sound.
Eels masquerade in disco light,
As sea stars break into a dance so bright.

The fish debate with bubbles high,
'Is the ocean blue or just shy?'
A catfish wears sunglasses tight,
While turtles snicker, what a sight!

Anchors drop with floppy grace,
As octopuses join the race.
With every splash, the giggles flow,
In currents strange, where nonsense grows.

Come ride the wave of laughter's tide,
In the silly depths where dreams collide!
The darkness hides all jokes, you see,
But the currents whisper, "Come laugh with me!"

Light's Defensive Retreat

When the glimmer dims and chuckles flee,
The glowworms hold a comedy spree.
With lanterns swaying to and fro,
They tell the jokes that only glow.

Flashlights flicker, slipping fast,
As shadows chase the fun they cast.
In the corners, giggles lurk,
In a game of hide and silly quirk.

The nighttime's laughter starts to wane,
While moonbeams tickle in the rain.
"A retreat!" says a firefly brave,
But he trips on a leaf, oh what a save!

So gather 'round, don't be dismayed,
In the light's retreat, let laughter cascade.
For though the darkness may draw near,
We dance with joy; there's nothing to fear!

Secrets of the Enshrouded

Beneath the ripples, whispers play,
Where secrets frolic, bright and gay.
Each bubble pops with tales so wild,
Of fish who act like cheeky child.

A turtle spills the gossip true,
Of mermaids wearing neon shoes.
Under the murky veil they spin,
With tales so zany, let the fun begin!

Eels make faces, crabby grins abound,
As sea snails shuffle, round and round.
In this deep nook, humor's embrace,
Where even the kelp can't hide its face.

Join the whispers of the deep,
Where laughter swells and secrets leap.
In the enshrouded, don't you drone,
For the best of jokes are found on loan!

Secrets Lurking in the Wetlands

Once a frog wore a crown, how absurd,
He'd croak out orders, not a word.
His subjects were ducks, all in a row,
They'd quack for laughter, putting on a show.

In the reeds, a raccoon danced, oh what a sight,
With a top hat and cane, he twirled in delight.
The turtles joined in, slow but proud,
Creating a spectacle, laughing out loud.

A fish with flair decided to sing,
He wore a bow tie, a jocular thing.
With bubbles and giggles, the party took flight,
In these secretive places, the fun felt just right.

So when you wander through the green,
Remember the laughter that's often unseen.
For in the wetlands, there's always a jest,
Just peek through the grasses, and you'll find the best.

Dreams Anchored in the Drift

A boat with no captain, just drifting along,
Sing songs to the wind, though they might be wrong.
A sock found its mate in a mystical stream,
Together they danced in a fanciful dream.

The clouds floated by like marshmallow fluff,
While a crab told jokes, in a voice oh so gruff.
He cracked up the gulls, who rolled in the air,
Chasing their giggles with not a single care.

Drifting through waters, dreams are a rip,
A turtle with shades took a leisurely trip.
He winked at the minnows, who swam with style,
In the currents of laughter, we'd linger a while.

So if you're adrift, don't you fret or pout,
For laughter and dreams are what life's about.
Just let the tide guide you with ease and with grit,
And find the humor where the shadows sit.

Murky Reflections of Timelessness

In a pond with no mirror, things seemed amiss,
Reflections of frogs were impossible bliss.
They leapt with such flair, in a splashy ballet,
While the lily pads cheered in a jubilant way.

A fish wore a wig, quite a sight to behold,
Telling tall tales of treasure and gold.
He winked at the catfish, both cracked up in glee,
As they plotted a heist for a magical spree.

The turtles discussed how old ponds could be,
As they reminisced about fish who drank tea.
With smiles on their faces, they embraced the day,
For in murky waters, laughter finds a way.

So dip in your toes and don't worry or frown,
For timeless reflections keep spinning around.
Join the antics of critters, and let your heart sing,
In the playful chaos, find joy in the spring.

The Hidden Mists of Twilight

As twilight descends, the fireflies appear,
A party of lights that brings everyone near.
The crickets are crooning a whimsical tune,
While raccoons in tuxedos dance under the moon.

A wise old owl hooted, "What's this all about?"
As frogs with umbrellas hopped in and out.
They twirled and they spun, they drank from a cup,
In the misty discussions, they giddily sup.

The breeze carried laughter, it tickled the night,
As the bushes conspired, plotting delight.
From hidden perspectives, the fun never waned,
In the mists where the silly and magical reigned.

So wander at dusk, let whimsy take flight,
For in those soft shrouds, you'll find pure delight.
Embrace all the antics, join the jovial throng,
In the hidden mists, it's where you belong.

Luminous Lore Beneath the Waves

Beneath the sea, where laughter hides,
A fish wears glasses, oh how he pried!
With bubble-gum coral, floating around,
Sea turtles chuckle, in silence profound.

Octopuses act like they're in a play,
With jiggly jelly, they dance and sway.
A crab throws a party, it's quite the spree,
But seahorses think they're too fancy, you see.

Clams tell tall tales of treasures untold,
Of pirate ships lost in waters so cold.
Mermaids gossip about what they wear,
While dolphins debate the best kind of hair!

In this below world, where quirkiness thrives,
Even the seaweed has fun jive vibes.
So come take a dive in this watery realm,
Where laughter's the helm and joy's at the helm!

The Remaining Echo

In the depths there lurks a grouchy old fish,
Who dreams of a world comprised of his dish.
Echoes of giggles swim past like a breeze,
While rays throw jokes that tumble with ease.

A clam shouts, 'Hey, I'm a real pearl!'
But every reply comes from a spinning whirl.
Shrimps play tag with their legs all a-flap,
In this watery circus, all wear a cap.

They host boat races with seaweed as flags,
With jellyfish cheering and turtley brags.
Eels do impressions of royalty's wail,
While squids scribble stories that drift with the sail.

All tales of the ocean rise with a cheer,
Where laughter's the treasure, and joy's ever near.
Each hint of a giggle that floats like a dream,
Is only the echo of the next silly scheme!

Forays into Submerged Dreams

Dipping into dreams where the sunlight glows,
A pufferfish joins in wearing pink bows.
Winking at starfish with a curious wink,
While snails pace softly, making you think.

Electric eels jolt with a zap and a zing,
Turning the tide into some wacky fling.
Barnacles dance on the rhythm of tides,
As crabs in tuxedos sway with their brides.

The sea lettuce giggles, swaying with grace,
Sardines gather round for a comedy race.
Anemones tease with tickles galore,
While fish share secrets of the ocean floor.

So float on this journey, embrace the delight,
Where laughter bubbles and dreamers take flight.
The depths hold a charm, a quirky embrace,
In the swirl of the tides, there's always a space!

Glimmering Touches of the Unknown

In the shimmer below, the funny fish blend,
With jokes that weave waters as currents suspend.
Crabs do the cha-cha, all clapping their claws,
While eels tell tall tales of their fanciest jaws.

The chorus of bubbles sings notes of pure glee,
Where clownfish perform with a fishy marquee.
Mollusks chuckle, their shells snug and bright,
While sea cucumbers just roll in delight.

A sea lion jokes with a nonchalant flair,
Saying, "What's the catch?" while tangling his hair.
The tides keep on laughing, it's really a show,
Where giggles and gleams put on quite the glow.

So wade in the waves, let your worries dismiss,
For beneath the blue, there's enchanting bliss.
Where silliness splashes in colors so bold,
The secrets of laughter in waters unfold!

Illusions of the Liquid Realm

Bubbles rise with a silly pop,
Goldfish wearing hats, they never stop.
The water sways like a dancing fool,
Who knew seaweed could bend the rule?

Marshmallow boats on a chocolate sea,
Sailors giggle, not one gloomy spree.
Octopus juggling, quite the delight,
Clams tell jokes that go all night.

A rainbow fish plays the ukulele,
With each pluck, everyone gets quite gaily.
Seahorses strut, a parade in their glow,
In this liquid realm, laughter will flow.

Look out for the mermaid in clown shoes,
Swimming past with absurd little views.
With every splash is a new funny line,
In this water realm, everything's divine.

Between Tomorrow and Yesterday

Time-traveling llamas on a wild spree,
Chasing rainbows and drinking their tea.
The clocks melt like ice, oh what a sight,
While turtles debate what day is right.

Yesterday's pancake flew through the air,
Landed on Tuesday, oh what to bear!
As tomorrow's donut rolls down the lane,
They laugh at the mess, but love the gain.

A cat thinks it's Wednesday, too soon for play,
But the mice have a party, they laugh and sway.
The fish in the pond giggle and gloat,
With every tick-tock, they float their boat.

Between now and then, the fun will abound,
With slip-ups and flops, smiles will be found.
Glimpses of giggles in time's quirky dance,
Life's just a joke, given half the chance.

Faint Ambushes from the Abyss

Creepy sea cucumbers plotting their tricks,
While jellyfish whisper their spooky flicks.
Ghostly snails wearing hats made of sea foam,
Seek out lost treasure, but they won't come home.

Waves giggle at krakens trying to hide,
In a game of peek-a-boo, they take pride.
Eels slackline between rocks, what a sight,
As tiny fish chuckle in sheer delight.

Sea urchins roll dice, who knew they could play?
Fishy gamblers, taking bets every day.
With bubbles of laughter rising below,
Faintly ambushed, it's a comedic show.

A squid in a hat, oh what a delight,
Causing a ruckus in depths outta sight.
When monsters get funny, life's far from grim,
In the abyss, the laughter won't dim.

A Glint Through the Dark

Navigating waters where silliness thrives,
A lighthouse beams where the silly ship dives.
With winks from the seaweed, the fish dance about,
Chasing each other, there's no room for doubt.

A wink from the starfish, a giggle from sand,
Surprises await where the fun is so grand.
Captain Clam sails with a grin on his face,
It's a treasure hunt mixed with a humorous race!

Watch out for the dolphin, he's cracking a joke,
Trying to hide a big, slippery poke.
Under the seabed, the laughter won't cease,
Every wave carries humor, a playful release.

Under a blanket of moon's silver light,
Creatures giggle as they swim through the night.
With each gentle splash, the dark's less profound,
A glint through the waters where joy can resound.

Ethereal Dreams on the Water's Edge

On the bank where the lilies sway,
A frog rehearses for its big play.
With a crown made of reeds, oh how it beams,
In a world that flows like forgotten dreams.

The fish are gossiping, full of cheer,
Telling tales of the guy in the weird sphere.
A turtle is chuckling, a sight to behold,
As it spins a yarn that's terribly bold.

The wind makes faces, sways tall grass,
Winks at the daisies, just let it pass.
Each splash and ripple bursts into laughter,
Creating a tale for the curious crafter.

As dusk wraps the scene in a cozy embrace,
Fireflies gather to dance and to chase.
If you listen closely, you might just hear,
The giggles of nature, oh so near!

Veils of Dusk

In a corner where the reeds pop out,
A squirrel dives in, with a flippity shout.
Eager to join the grand evening show,
It twirls and it swirls with an overblown 'whoa!'

The sun dips low, painting skies in pink,
A fish pokes its head and gives a sly wink.
With its fin raised high, it starts a parade,
Marshmallows are scattered, delightful charade!

The chattering crickets join in the play,
Making sweet music till the light fades away.
A turtle orchestrates with a stick of old wood,
Leading the creatures, all feeling so good.

As laughter spills over the soft night tide,
The antics of nature can't be denied.
What joy it brings, this wacky delight,
With creatures and quirks tucked in the night!

Echoes Beneath the Surface

Beneath the waves where the sillies reside,
A fish brags loudly, oh what a pride!
With sequined scales, it dances and shines,
Claiming it's the star of the underwater lines.

A clam retorts with a pinch of salt,
"You're not the best, just look at your vault!"
The seaweed chuckles, free-spirited and spry,
While bubbles of laughter float up to the sky.

Octopuses spin tales, quite tangled and fun,
As they juggle with sea urchins, one by one.
Laughs resonate through the briny deep,
Echoes of whimsy, secrets to keep.

As beams of the moon make the currents twirl,
They dance to the rhythm, give laughter a whirl.
Freedom is found just beneath the foam,
Where giggles and chuckles make the sea home!

Whispers of the Undercurrent

In the brook where the minnows flit around,
A vole pops by, curious and profound.
It tickles the water with a dainty toe,
And giggles out loud at the silly show.

The lilypads giggle, with such fine flair,
As the wind tousles them without a care.
A heron takes note, gives a sly little grin,
Guess it's the fish who are ready to swim!

Bubbles escape with a plinky little sound,
A turtle in pajamas scouts the ground.
Throwing a bash with its algae-filled friends,
The fun never halts, it wobbles and bends!

In the twilight glow, with a promise of cheer,
Nature's an artist, creating sincere.
Whispers of laughter in water run wild,
Bringing out joy, like a playful child!

Murmurs in the Silent Depths

Bubbles giggle in low tones,
Fish tell tales of safety cones.
Crabs dance funny, pinch and sway,
Clams gossip 'bout the light of day.

Octopus wearing polka dots,
Waves of laughter 'neath the knots.
Seashells chat in whispers soft,
Mermaids snicker, dreams aloft.

Mermen juggle with seaweed rings,
Turtles swoosh like roller skates kings.
Eels masquerade in fancy dress,
Tickling tails, oh what a mess!

With chuckles bouncing off the reef,
Underwater joy beyond belief.
Giggling gulls above take flight,
Funny fish dance into the night.

Phantoms of the Moonlit Bay

Under the moon, a prankster swell,
Ghostly figures in a poor shell.
They slip and slide, trying to glide,
Chortling softly in the tide.

A jellyfish wearing a top hat bold,
Tells fishy jokes that never get old.
Barnacles join, to toe-tap tunes,
Giggling loudly, beneath the moons.

Whispers of pirates, tales of clums,
Foggy forms and their silly drums.
Crabs in wigs, with skittering feet,
Dancing the night with shimmery beat.

Echoes of laughter bounce in the air,
Silly spectres, without a care.
Under the moon, they find their play,
In the haunted bay, they joke away.

Secrets of the Sunken Veil

There's a caper in the kelp green,
Fish telling secrets, rarely seen.
Octopus eyes widening with glee,
Unraveling knots for a cup of tea.

A seahorse sporting a tiny crown,
Flipping and flopping, never a frown.
Clownfish teasing with their red stripes,
Spilling laughter, no stereotypes.

Buried treasures, oh such surprise,
Gems that giggle in disguise.
Squids write jokes in ink on a stone,
Snickering softly, never alone.

Weaving tales through ocean's choir,
Silly secrets that never tire.
Under the waves, where chuckles soar,
Sunken wonders forevermore.

Flickers of Light in Dark Waters

Glowing critters with tiny lights,
Dance around in silly flights.
Flickering laughter, soft and bright,
In the deep, they share their delight.

A fish with a giggle, bubbles galore,
Flicks its tail, asking for more.
Worms in hats plotting their schemes,
Underneath, where nothing's as it seems.

Crickets chirp in gurgling tones,
Underwater, they share their moans.
Ticklish tugs from the seaweed loom,
Every corner filled with humor's bloom.

Glorious gleams in the watery night,
Radiant quirks that feel just right.
In the depths where the fun is tight,
Joy flickers on, a glittering sight.

Hemmed by Haze

In the mist where the fish play,
I tripped over my own way.
With a splash and a jolly shout,
I grew gills, there's no doubt!

Bubbles danced like they were aware,
Of all the laughter in the air.
A crab joined in with a cheeky grin,
Said, "Who invited you in?"

The seaweed laughed with a rustling sound,
As I swirled round and round.
Caught in the tide's silly embrace,
I tumbled through jellyfish space!

Then the octopus waved hello,
While wearing a hat of bright glow.
"Want to join my fancy soiree?"
I asked, "Is that sea cucumber okay?"

Songs of the Silent Depths

Beneath the waves where no one peeks,
The fish are gossiping for weeks.
With jokes about the crabby king,
They giggle, oh how they sing!

Anemones sway to their tune,
While a clownfish juggles a spoon.
The water's a stage, laughter so light,
Who knew loafers could take flight?

With bubbles that pop like surprise,
And a snail sporting a disguise,
Every creature wears a silly grin,
In the depths where the fun begins!

So come for a dance on the ocean bed,
It's a bash for all—no one's misled.
Forget your worries and join the jest,
Under the waves, we're clearly blessed!

Echoes of the Shimmering Edge

At twilight's brink, the seagulls caw,
As the dolphins share tales of awe.
They pirouette 'round the glowing light,
Who knew plankton could be so bright?

A lobster's dressed in a fancy suit,
Dancing to the rhythm, none can dispute.
With a twist of a fin and a flip of a tail,
He tells tales that are sure to prevail!

The seafoam chuckles at their parade,
As fish throw confetti and shade.
"Let's start the party, don't be late!"
Echoes of fun—the sea's first date!

Sunset whispers secrets so sweet,
In the company of friends, life's a treat.
Under water's charm, we all unite,
For giggles and grace till the morning light!

Pondering the In-Between

Between the tides where mischief brews,
The crabs wear spectacles, not a ruse.
They discuss clams who keep the time,
While dancing on pearls, oh so sublime!

A seahorse shares his latest chore,
Hitching rides on a turtle's floor.
Together they plot a whimsical scheme,
A race to catch the seaweed dream!

The starfish plays a game of chess,
With an eel who loves to impress.
"Oh, you're too slow!" the shore critters shout,
Yet giggles arise with every clout!

Here in the water where fun's the law,
Creatures delight in the wonders they saw.
In the swirls of life, they leap, they sway,
Oh, to be a finned friend every day!

The Quiet Lurkers of the Lagoon

In the lagoon where silence reigns,
Fish gossip in invisible chains.
Crabs wear hats made of seaweed green,
Whispering secrets, unseen and keen.

A turtle giggles, trying to hide,
Under a leaf, it feels quite spry.
"Did you see that jump!" the fish declare,
A splash of fun hangs in the air.

Oysters grin with their pearly shells,
Sharing tales that nobody tells.
With bubbles popping, they laugh and roar,
As lizards dance on the sandy shore.

So when you visit their watery haunt,
Remember the fun they all can flaunt.
In quiet corners, life's a play,
With sliding smiles to light the day.

Elusive Forms of the Coastal Realm

In the twilight where shapes do sway,
Sandy figures play in a silly way.
A starfish spins, a comical sight,
Making waves with all its might.

Seagulls squawk in hilarious tones,
Diving low, they bump the stones.
A crab in shades throws a beach bash,
It scuttles sideways with a dash.

A jellyfish floats, like a disco ball,
In rhythmic moves, it invites us all.
"Join the dance!" a clam starts to sing,
While the waves applaud this crazy fling.

With laughter echoing through the tide,
These playful spirits get crazy wide.
In coastal realms, where beings meet,
A silly party can't be beat!

Veils of Mist in the Estuary

In an estuary where mist likes to dance,
Silhouetted shapes play a wild romance.
A heron jests with a twig in its beak,
While fish chase bubbles, like hide-and-seek.

Otters tumble in a swirling spree,
Rolling and splashing, happy as can be.
"Catch that wave!" one shouts in delight,
As a sneaky ray gives them a fright.

The fog rolls in with a sneaky grin,
Lifting its veil, letting the fun begin.
"Mist-covered giggles," the frogs croak loud,
As they hop about, feeling oh so proud.

So if you wander through the quiet mist,
Know that between folly and bliss,
Lurking within the soft gray swells,
Are playful spirits, do tell the tales.

Fleeting Visions of Tidal Whispers

In whispers soft that lap the shore,
Beneath the tide, adventures soar.
Tiny fish laugh as they dart in a line,
Playing tag with the porpoise, oh so fine.

The sun sets low with a mischievous grin,
Painting the water like a whimsical spin.
Crabs in the sand hold their laughter tight,
As they jive to the rhythm in fading light.

An octopus winks from beneath a stone,
Dancing alone, in colors well-known.
"Come play with me!" it shouts with glee,
As the tide pulls back, so wild and free.

The night creeps in, like a cheeky thief,
But laughter echoes, bringing relief.
For in every wave, a giggle remains,
In playful moments, the joy never wanes.

www.ingramcontent.com/pod-product-compliance
Lightning Source LLC
Chambersburg PA
CBHW060121230426
43661CB00003B/282